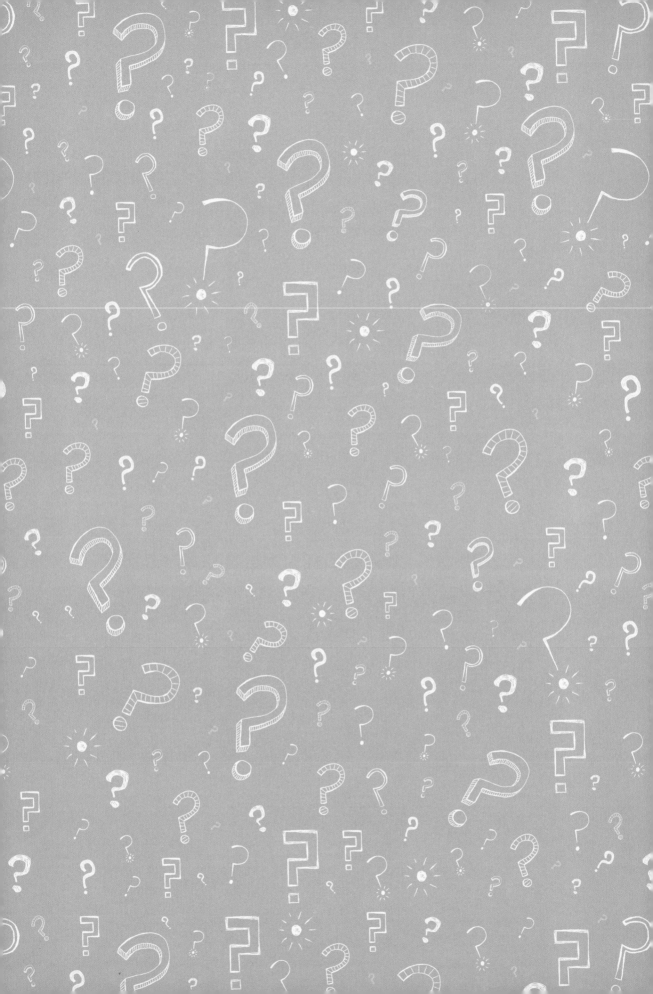

WHY is ART full of NAKED PEOPLE?

& other vital questions about art

WHY is ART full of NAKED PEOPLE?

& other vital questions about art

Written by **Susie Hodge**

Original illustrations by **Claire Goble**

Thames & Hudson

CONTENTS

WHY SO MANY QUESTIONS?

Where do artists get their ideas from? Can you show feelings in pictures? Why is some art so weird?

Perhaps you've asked some of these things when you've visited an art gallery? If so that's good, because asking questions can help you to understand what an artist is trying to say and why a piece of work makes you feel a particular way. Art is meant to make us think in new ways.

Did you know that artists ask themselves many questions while they're making their work too? It helps them to create something new and different. In this book you'll have the chance to explore lots of questions about art.

Belshazzar's Feast, Rembrandt, 1635

What gave the artist this idea?

Rembrandt wanted to paint something familiar in a new way. In Rembrandt's time, everyone knew the stories of the Bible. But no one had seen Belshazzar's Feast painted so vividly before! Rembrandt captures the most dramatic moment, when wicked King Belshazzar is warned that he will die. Look how terrified everyone is of the floating hand writing the warning on the wall.

How do you make art scary?

Before Edvard Munch painted this, most artists tried to make their art look realistic.

But Munch decided to paint his feelings in a way that he thought would be more powerful than a lifelike picture. So he used strong contrasting colors, wild, waving lines and a skull-like face that's quite scary! It might seem to be a simple image, but it makes you want to ask a lot of questions. Is that a sunset or blood? Are those two figures walking towards us or away? Why is he screaming?

The Scream. Edvard Munch. 1893

Why paint shapes?

What's this painting about and what are we supposed to think about it?

Well, it's up to you! In this painting Kazimir Malevich didn't include people, stories or still lifes on purpose. He didn't even try to make things look like real objects. Instead, he painted simple shapes, patterns and colors. Do you think these shapes are floating or falling?

Suprematist Composition. Kazimir Malevich. 1916

Are STICK MEN ART?

HOW → many deer can you find?

Not all people in works of art are made to look REALISTIC.

Sometimes artists draw people as stick figures on purpose. And it's not because they can't draw!

Some artists want to **tell stories** that can be **understood quickly**. Others want their pictures to **grab people's attention**. Simple figures are often the best way to do this.

Artists might want to show people in a general way **without personal details**, such as facial features, or even clothes. Many artists want to show **personalities**, **moods** or **expressions**, and they feel that they can do it better with **simple figures** than with more detailed pictures.

Rock painting from Utah, USA, artist unknown, c. 150 CE

These **stick figures** were drawn on a rock in Utah almost 2000 years ago. They are called **petroglyphs**. Artists used **hand-made tools** to **scratch simple** pictures on to the surface of the rocks, revealing lighter-colored rock underneath.

They tell **stories** of **Native American tribesmen** hunting deer, buffalo and antelope on horseback.

Find out about stories in art
Go to page 28

BOUNCE!

Does this picture remind you of a cartoon? Keith Haring learned how to draw from his dad, who drew comic strips for a living.

A lot of people say that cartoons aren't "real" art, but Haring wanted to make sure that everyone understood his pictures instantly. His straightforward figures grab our attention and everyone understands them. Full of energy and action, this bouncy man is Haring's way of showing that the world needs lively people to sort out all its problems!

Untitled. Keith Haring, 1982

SPOT THE DIFFERENCE!

LS Lowry painted simple, stick-like figures so that he could make them all look the same.

Here, factory workers swarm towards the gates at the start of a working day. They look like worker ants. Lowry shows how similar we all are — we all wake up, go to work (or school), go home, and go to bed.

Going to Work. LS Lowry, 1959

IS THIS MAN IN CONTROL?

Alberto Giacometti wanted to show people's personalities in the simplest way. He was interested in human nature rather than physical likenesses. When he made a sculpture of someone, he stripped away all the detail.

By making sculptures thin and without detail he believed that he could show their inner feelings. Do you think this man is confident and in control, or shy and quiet?

Man Pointing, Alberto Giacometti, 1947

11

Are there any UGLY STATUES?

Most sculptures have been made to look BEAUTIFUL.

This began with the **ancient Greeks** who insisted that artists make everything look **lifelike**, but **perfect**. They believed that certain distances and measurements, or **proportions**, show **"ideal" beauty,** which is not necessarily "real." So in ancient Greek art, **no one ever looks old, ugly or fat.**

LOOK at how perfectly balanced this athlete is!

An **ancient Greek athlete** is about to throw the discus. This sculpture captures a moment of action. The man's muscular body sums up the **Greek idea of perfection**. The ancient Greeks invented the Olympic Games. To them, their **Olympic athletes** were **perfect** humans. This is one of the most famous sculptures from ancient times.

Why is art full of naked people?
Go to page 24

Discobolus Lancellotti, Roman copy after a bronze original by Myron, 460-450 BCE

WHAT A FACE!

"My art is childlike," Karel Appel once said. He often created quite frightening, cartoon-like objects in bright, bold colors.

Appel belonged to an art group in which all the artists tried to think like children as they made their paintings and objects. Their art often turned out to be quite ugly as they tried to show the world in a different way.

Karel Appel. Mouse on Table, 1971

ONE FACE OR TWO?

Pablo Picasso thought that by making sculptures from more than one viewpoint he could show more of his subjects than if he made them from just one angle.

The results often look quite strange! Do you think this face looks odd, even ugly? That's because some parts of her face are shown from different angles all at the same time.

Head of a Woman. Pablo Picasso, 1962

DOES SHE LOOK CARING?

She might not look beautiful or like a person you know. But as this figure lies back and relaxes, do you see a warm, kind person that you might be able to rely on, or who you could lean against when you're tired?

Henry Moore made this simple, curving shape to capture his idea of a woman. Round forms usually suggest kindness and capability.

Recumbent Figure. Henry Moore, 1938

All PICTURES are in FRAMES - aren't they?

LOOK →

Do you think this painting should be in a frame?

Usually paintings are framed to SHOW THEM OFF.

Frames draw attention to the picture inside and protect the edges. Some are rather **elaborate**, especially for art that was made to be displayed in grand houses long ago. Other frames can be quite **simple and plain**, so they don't distract you from the art. But frames are always designed to **complement**, or to finish off, the artwork inside, to make it **look better** in some way.

Composition with Yellow, Red, Black, Blue and Gray, Piet Mondrian, 1920

Piet Mondrian thought that **frames** were **like walls**. Sometimes they seemed to stand between viewers and art, as if they **blocked**, or separated, paintings from the **rest of the world**. Mondrian wanted everyone to enjoy his work, and no one to feel **separated** from it. So he painted right to the **edge** of his canvases. Sometimes he painted on the sides of the canvas too. He **knocked down those walls!**

Can you make a frame out of a box?
Look on page 74

A PAINTED FRAME!

Georges Seurat didn't like the way that picture frames create shadows around the edges of paintings. So he painted one instead. This frame is made up of thousands of tiny dots around the edges of the canvas. It was made from over 25 different colors.

Did you know that the picture on your TV screen is made up of lots of tiny dots called pixels? This picture was painted over 50 years before the color TV was invented!

A Sunday Afternoon on the Island of La Grande Jatte. Georges Seurat. 1884

THIS PICTURE IS CALLED "THE FRAME"!

In this self-portrait, Frida Kahlo uses a frame to grab her viewers' attention. You can't miss the bright colors in the border around her face.

The colors, birds and flowers show us things from Kahlo's Mexican background, suggesting the sunny climate and beautiful surroundings of her country. With the same yellow in her hair and around her neck that's in the frame, you can't help but look at her face.

The Frame, Frida Kahlo, 1938

HEAVENLY?

When this picture was painted, there was no electricity. It was made for a dark cathedral lit by candles. The gold frame caught the flickering light, making it look magical and heavenly.

The decorations on the frame made it look grand, showing that the work was about important figures in the Bible. The Angel Gabriel is telling the Virgin Mary that she will be the mother of Jesus.

Annunciation with St Margaret and St Ansanus, Simone Martini and Lippo Memmi, 1333

WHY is everything FLAT?

WHAT → is Nebamun doing?

Some art doesn't try to make things look 3D.

Two-dimensions, or **2D, means flat,** like this page. Three-dimensions, or **3D,** means anything that has **height, width and depth,** like a ball.

At different times and places, painters have tried to make their art look either as flat as the surfaces they paint on or 3D, like real objects.

Lots of **ancient art**, such as this Egyptian wall painting, **looks flat.** It is more **like a diagram** than a picture, and not meant to look **lifelike**.

Since ancient times, artists have discovered how to make art look 3D, or they've painted their pictures to **look flat on purpose**.

Nebamun Fowling in the Marshes.
Tomb-chapel of Nebamun, c. 1350 BCE

Important people in **ancient Egypt** were buried in **painted tombs** full of treasures. The wall art in their tombs was not made to be seen by the living. It was created to **show the gods** what people had done during their lives.

The picture **looks flat** so that the gods could **understand it easily.**

Are stick men art?
Go to page 8

21

This painting by Sophie Taeuber-Arp is not pretending to be something else, like a tree or a portrait. The picture is simply flat shapes, lines and colors made with paint. It is all about flatness.

Taeuber-Arp also designed textiles, which helped her to realize that there is no rule that says paintings have to look three-dimensional.

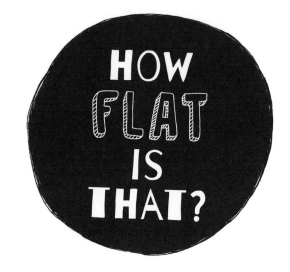

Untitled. Sophie Taeuber-Arp, 1932

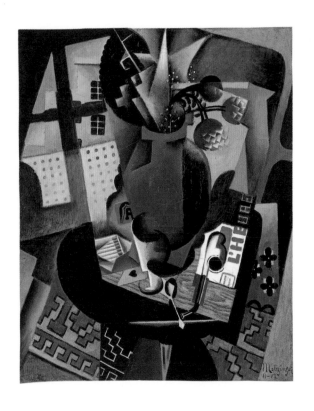

HOW MANY VIEWPOINTS?

What's on the table? Can you see a vase of flowers, a glass, a playing card and a window?

Jean Metzinger didn't follow the usual rules of perspective, but still wanted to show that the things in his picture were 3D. So he painted everything from different angles, or viewpoints, at the same time. This technique is called Cubism.

Table by a Window, Jean Metzinger, 1917

A REAL FACE OR A MASK?

Amedeo Modigliani wanted to capture people's personalities, not make them look like photographs. All his sitters look flat, with long necks and almond-shaped eyes.

Modigliani believed that by making his paintings flat and stylized, he showed people's inner characters more than their outward appearances.

What do you think this woman is thinking about? Can you tell what her personality is like?

Woman with a Fan, Amedeo Modigliani, 1919

WHY is ART full of NAKED PEOPLE?

Naked people are absolutely EVERYWHERE in paintings, sculptures and photographs.

It all started with the **ancient Greeks** who thought that the **naked body** was **beautiful** and should be studied.

Even today artists **train** by drawing naked people to help understand the **form**, or shape, of the body. It is called **life drawing**.

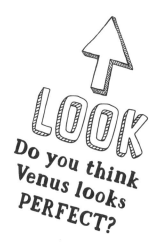

LOOK
Do you think Venus looks PERFECT?

Venus, the Roman **goddess of love and beauty,** is stark naked floating on a seashell. In the ancient story, Venus was born grown-up and she rode on a seashell on the sea. Botticelli painted her many years after the story was first told.

In art, nakedness often stands for new life. In Botticelli's time, real women covered themselves up. But it was fine to paint Venus naked because she was a **perfect goddess**, not a **real woman**!

The Birth of Venus, Sandro Botticelli, 1486

Are there any ugly statues?
Go to page 12

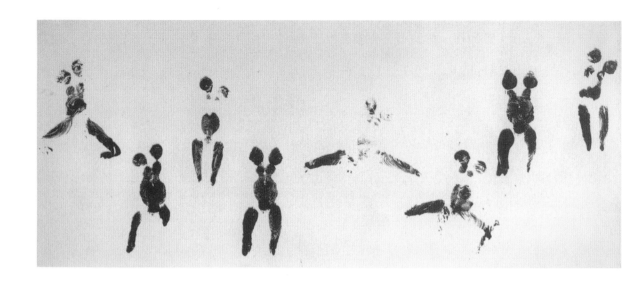

WHY SO MANY NAKED WOMEN?

Many artists have thought that the female body is more beautiful than the male body, so naked women appear in art more often than naked men.

In 1960, Yves Klein explored new ways of painting female bodies. He covered naked women in blue paint then laid them on a huge canvas on the floor. He was using the women's bodies as "living paintbrushes."

BUT THEY'RE NOT NAKED!

Sometimes it's interesting to ask why artists show people with their clothes on. Grant Wood painted this picture in 1930 in the Midwest, where being naked was embarrassing. These are hard-working farmers, not gods and goddesses. Perhaps their buttoned-up clothes help to show how they looked at the world. What do you think?

American Gothic, Grant Wood, 1930

A naked woman is at a picnic with two men wearing clothes. At the time this was painted, people were horrified. It was too shocking! Édouard Manet didn't understand what all the fuss was about. Why was it OK to paint naked people as gods and goddesses, but not ordinary people doing everyday things?

Look at the naked woman. She's staring right back at you, the viewer!

Le Déjeuner sur l'Herbe (The Luncheon on the Grass), Édouard Manet, 1863

ARE YOU OUTRAGED BY THIS PICTURE?

WHAT'S the STORY?

Stories are told in ALL SORTS
OF ART - from painting and
sculpture to video and film.

When we look at art, we are given
a **window** into another person's
imagination. We can see **facts** and
stories through **someone else's eyes**.

About 160 years ago, there was an
art movement called the **Pre-Raphaelite
Brotherhood** where artists painted **stories**,
often from **history**. Their paintings were
sometimes nicknamed "**novels in frames**."
Millais was a Pre-Raphaelite artist.

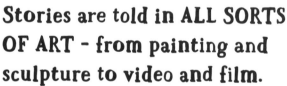

REALLY?

Millais made
his model lie
fully clothed in a
bathtub of water.
She caught
a cold!

This painting is of **Ophelia**, a character in Hamlet, a play by **William Shakespeare**. The beautiful, sad Ophelia drowned. Here, the **artist imagines** how it might have happened. He includes lots of **symbols** to make the painting more **interesting**. For example, the red poppies and blue forget-me-nots stand for **remembrance,** or remembering the dead.

This was a **well-known story** and people flocked to see the painting at the Royal Academy in London when it was first displayed in 1852.

Ophelia. John Everett Millais, 1851-52

Does art make you clever?
Go to page 84

Cold Dark Matter: An Exploded View,
Cornelia Parker, 1991

This piece of art tells a story of a different kind. Cornelia Parker wanted to create a mood, or atmosphere, to make us think about our lives and what we leave behind at the end of them.

A garden shed is something many of us see without thinking much about, and something lots of people fill up with things they forget about. Parker decided to blow one up!

She then took all the bits of charred wood and twisted metal and hung them from the ceiling with invisible thread. A light bulb was placed in the center to create eerie shadows on the walls.

The Bayeux tapestry is a famous and extremely long piece of embroidery. (The length of three swimming pools!) It includes fifty scenes, which tell the story of a real event — the Norman invasion of England in 1066. Here, the Normans are charging forward on their horses, wearing armor and chain mail, carrying bows and arrows.

The Bayeux Tapestry (detail), c. 1070

A GAME OF CHESS?

Some paintings tell us about a person's life or a time in history. Here, the artist has painted her sisters playing a game of chess. Their maid stands behind. In those days it was unusual for girls to be educated or to become artists. But these girls were daughters of a wealthy nobleman and we know they've been educated because they can play chess!

The Chess Game, Sofonisba Anguissola, 1555

31

WHO are ALL these PEOPLE?

Art is jam-packed with people, but WHO are they all?

In the past, before **photography** was invented, many important people had their **portraits** painted. Artists were expected to show how **powerful, beautiful, rich** or **handsome** these people were. Often, whole families were painted in one large portrait.

Sometimes, artists also painted themselves to make **self-portraits.**

WHO → is in the mirror?

It's a crowded room and a **royal portrait**. The little blonde girl in the center is Margarita Teresa, the five-year-old daughter of the King and Queen of Spain. The artist, **Velázquez**, has included himself in the painting, so it is also a **self-portrait**. He is painting the King and Queen, who are standing where we are. Can you find them?

Las Meninas, Diego Velázquez, 1656

Edward Hopper's portrait is of two fashionable ladies having lunch. Unlike the subjects of portraits of the past, these women are not powerful or important. They are just ordinary, and could be anyone sitting in a restaurant. When we're out in crowds we see lots of people we don't know at all and that's what Hopper wanted to paint.

Even though he was showing us two strangers, both women were modeled by Hopper's wife!

THEY'RE NOT IMPORTANT!

Chop Suey, Edward Hopper, 1929

A GRUESOME SIGHT!

This picture tells the Bible story of David and Goliath. David killed the murderous giant with just a stone and a sling. Caravaggio copied his own face to paint Goliath's severed head.

Why do you think he painted himself as a monstrous giant? Perhaps it was just because he was cheaper than an artist's model. Or maybe he felt that he too, could be scary like Goliath!

David with the Head of Goliath,
Caravaggio, 1610

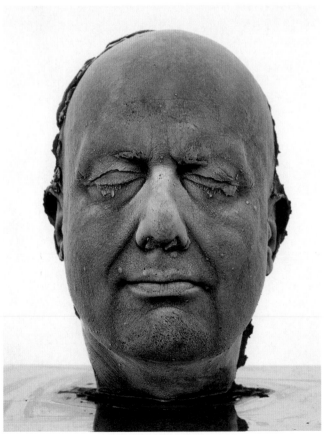

This is a self-portrait of the artist made out of himself! Marc Quinn used his own blood to fill a cast, or mold, of his head. It must be kept frozen or it will melt.

Quinn says it's a reminder of how fragile life is. He makes a new version every five years, so you can see him ageing.

Self. Marc Quinn, 2006

35

WHAT'S with all the FRUIT?

Artists are always painting apples and oranges, but WHY?

First off, fruit is **reliable**. Unlike a human model, it won't blink or twitch or want a cup of tea.

Painting fruit also **helps artists to learn** about shapes, colors and tones in nature.

These paintings are called **still life paintings** because, well, they're **still**!

Before the invention of **photography**, artists showed off their skills with realistic still life paintings. But afterwards, things changed...

FRUIT 'N' VEG

LOOK

Cézanne said "I will astonish Paris with an apple!" What did he mean?

Paul Cézanne painted this picture
after the camera was invented, so he
didn't feel that he needed to make it
realistic. A photograph could do that!

He painted round fruit on a flat
canvas, but in a new way. To help
show the **true shapes** and **forms** of the
fruit, he painted each apple from lots
of **different angles** and **viewpoints** all
at once. It makes the apples look like
they're about to **fall off the table**.

Apples and Oranges. Paul Cézanne, 1899

Who else
painted lots
of viewpoints
all at once?
Go to page 60

A bunch of flowers explodes! Our eyes couldn't see this moment in real life because it happens too fast. But the camera can freeze it in time.

The artist based this photograph on a still life painting from the 1800s.

Just think, the first still life paintings were realistic and detailed because there was no photography, while this still life uses photography to show something that no artist could ever see!

Blow Up 05. Ori Gersht. 2007

A **SKULL** & **FRUIT** – REALLY?

This painting is all about double meanings. Jan van Kessel has painted flowers, but also a skull, which stands for death. It's a warning that reminds us of the "vanity" of life. We shouldn't get too full of ourselves – in the end we all die!

The French name for still life, "nature morte," means dead nature. In the painting, the flowers look alive, but in real life time passes and flowers rot away to nothing.

Vanitas Still Life, Jan van Kessel, 1665-70

CAN A STILL LIFE BE ALIVE?

Yes – when the artist is a performance artist. Johan Lorbeer is also an optical illusionist who stars in his own still life work.

It's all rather puzzling. He's the subject, which means he's like the fruit in a still life painting, but he's alive and not made of paint! But then again, he's still and he hangs on a wall like a painting while time passes.

Tarzan/Standing Leg, Johan Lorbeer, 2002

WHY paint a VIEW?

So many LANDSCAPES!

For centuries, people have painted scenes of **fields, cities and mountains**.

But it was only around 300 years ago that landscapes on their own became **important in art**. This was thanks to a simple **invention** – the **paint tube**! Suddenly paints could be carried around wherever artists wanted to go, and it was easy to **paint in the open air**.

WHAT →

do YOU think HE is thinking about?

A man stands staring at the sea in front of him. This painting is as much **about the man** as it is about the landscape.

Caspar David Friedrich's landscape shows the **power of nature**. The man has his back towards us, so we can see the **same view** that he's seeing. The wild weather stretches out in front of him. It looks **mysterious** and a **bit alarming**.

Wanderer Above the Sea of Fog. Caspar David Friedrich, 1818

IS ART ON A TABLET REAL ART?

Why not? Just because artists didn't use them in the past, doesn't mean it's not art. It's just a new way of making art.

This is a wood near where David Hockney grew up. The picture is bright and colorful, just like Hockney's memories of his childhood.

Smartphones and tablets create super bright colors that can't always be made with paint.

The Arrival of Spring in Woldgate, East Yorkshire, David Hockney, 2011

WRAPPED UP!

Art about landscape doesn't always have to be in 2D. Christo and Jeanne-Claude wrapped 603,870 square metres of pink fabric around 11 islands in Miami.

The fabric was sewn into 79 patterns to follow the contours, or outlines, of the islands.

The pink cloth looked bright and bold against the blue water and the green vegetation.

Surrounded Islands, Biscayne Bay, Greater Miami, Florida, 1980-83, Christo and Jeanne-Claude, 1980-83

Not all landscape art is about the landscape! Sometimes, like this piece, it's about something else.

Agnes Denes' work is about how the landscape can feed everyone. Over many months, she planted wheat in an empty space in the middle of busy New York City. When it was harvested, the grain was sent to 28 other cities around the world where it was planted to remind people about hunger in the world.

Wheatfield – a Confrontation. Agnes Denes, 1982

WHY is everything BLURRY?

Some art is just MESSY!

Lots of artists paint with **untidy brushmarks** and **thick paint** splodged on. Many sculptors don't try to make their work smooth or neat. There are photographers who deliberately **blur** their images, too.

Artists have always **experimented**, but messiness became more common after **photography was invented** in 1839. Why make things look realistic when photos could do that?

Do you think she needs more details?

Berthe Morisot was an **Impressionist,** a group of painters who used **brisk, sketchy** brushstrokes. The Impressionists aimed to capture the **effects of light,** painting exactly what they saw in front of them quickly.

The **blurriness** developed partly from what they learned about light from photography, but also because these painters wanted to show how **different** painting could be from **photography.**

In the Dining Room. Berthe Morisot, 1886

JMW Turner created the effects of wild weather with smudged paint marks and no details. It is easy to imagine being in his small steamboat in the heart of a swirling snowstorm.

Turner painted with messy marks and thick layers of color on top of each other to create the feeling of being in an icy, whirling blizzard. A lot of people thought he was cheating by not painting details. But soon, most realized that this was a clever way of capturing the feeling of being in the middle of a wild tempest at sea.

WHAT CAN YOU SEE THROUGH THE STORM?

Steamboat off a Harbour's Mouth. JMW Turner, 1842

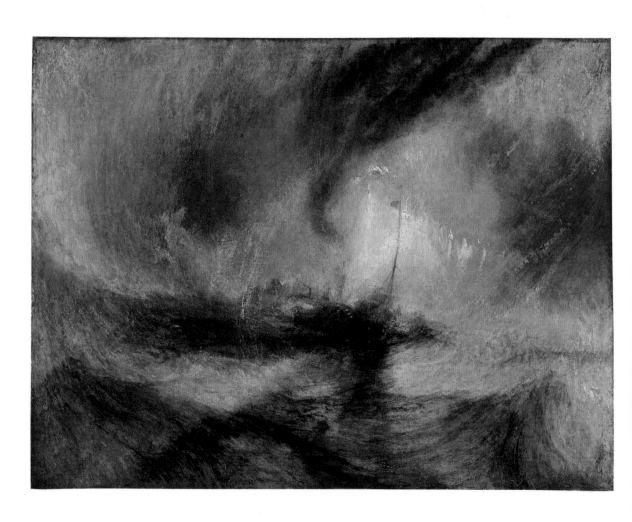

OUT OF FOCUS!

This painting is based on a blurred photo — the photographer moved while taking it. Gerhard Richter used this photo on purpose to show activity in a still image. Almost the opposite of a still life, the picture is not easy to understand because the four people seem to be in different places all at once.

Reisebüro (Tourist Office), Gerhard Richter, 1966

NOT BLURRY AT ALL!

Meredith Frampton painted this portrait with precise details, in a highly finished style. At the time, it was fashionable for artists to paint more expressively, with sketchy marks and sploshy paint. But Frampton didn't want to do this. He used tiny, almost invisible brush strokes and careful shading to create a soft, realistic image. Do you think it looks like a photograph?

A Game of Patience (Miss Margaret Austin-Jones), Meredith Frampton, 1937

Are there SPOTS before YOUR EYES?

There are a lot of DOTS in art!
They seem to be everywhere, from **teensy** printed or painted dots to **huge** spots and **3D balls**. Some artists even use **pixels**, the tiny dots that make up pictures on TV and computer screens.

Probably the best-known dotty art is **pointillism**, where artists paint with the **tips of their brushes**. Painters, such as Seurat and Signac, discovered that lots of little **spots and dots** can be used to make **gradual changes in tones and colors**.

IMAGINE if everything around you was covered in dots!

Yayoi Kusama really does see **spots before her eyes**. Since she was a little girl, she has had hallucinations, or seen **visions**, often of dots. She makes dotty art to show people how the world looks through her eyes. How does this picture **make you feel?** Kusama says her work can make people feel **positive and energetic**. She makes spotty paintings, collages, sculptures and installations, and she loves **bright colors**.

With All My Love For The Tulips, I Pray Forever, Yayoi Kusama, 2012

Is it upside down? Go to page 60

GOING DOTTY

In 1886, Georges Seurat and his friend Paul Signac invented a new way of painting. While most other painters mixed colors on palettes, they used small brushes to paint tiny colored dots in pure, unmixed colors. Seurat discovered that if you do this, when you stand back, your eyes mix the colors. The style is called pointillism because of the "points" of color. See how soft this painting looks, made of just dots and no hard lines.

Young Woman Powdering Herself. Georges Seurat, 1889-90

ARE THESE SPOTS MOVING?

How do you feel when you look at this picture by Bridget Riley? Is it moving or are you?

In the 1960s, Riley began painting images that make our eyes play tricks on us. This type of art is called "Op art," which comes from the term "optical illusions." Op art is not about what we see, but how we see it. It's all to do with geometry, shapes, colors and patterns and the way we see images. So you might think the spots are moving, but they're not!

Pause. Bridget Riley, 1964

Roy Lichtenstein was inspired by dots too. As part of the Pop art movement, he painted huge cartoon pictures, which are like giant printed comics from the 1940s and 1950s.

Just like in the comics, Lichtenstein spaced dots close together or far apart to give the effect of different colors and tones. Look at this picture from the other side of the room. Can you still see all the dots?

M-Maybe. Roy Lichtenstein, 1965

Is it FINISHED?

It can be HARD TO TELL if a piece of art is finished or not.

Sometimes artists leave their work unfinished, and later, it becomes admired as a **completed work**. Some art is **not unfinished** at all, but just **looks like it is!**

From around the 1500s until today, all around the world, a lot of art has been made that **looks incomplete.**

LOOK

at the way the figures are grouped together.

Leonardo da Vinci made this drawing over 500 years ago using charcoal and black and white chalk on eight sheets of paper glued together.

It may have been a design for a painting that he never did or that has **been lost**, but it is now admired as work of art in its own right, and that of **a genius**.

Look at the incredible detail in the dark and light tones, and the folds in the clothes!

The Virgin and Child with St Anne and St John the Baptist, Leonardo da Vinci, c. 1499–1500

RECOGNIZE THIS?

When Gilbert Stuart painted this portrait of George Washington in the late 1700s, he left it unfinished on purpose.

This was long before photography was invented. Stuart knew that if he finished the portrait, the president would want it. If he didn't finish it, he could keep it and use it to remind himself what Washington looked like. Despite being unfinished, the portrait is now really famous. It's been on American one-dollar bills for over a century!

George Washington, Gilbert Stuart, 1796

WHAT'S UNDERNEATH?

This is a finished painting, but people thought it wasn't. The sails aren't painted and you can see the canvas. André Derain did this deliberately. He wanted to show the canvas because it's the same material as real sails. He also thought that if he painted all of the canvas the picture would be boring, but if he painted in patchy marks, it would look lively.

The Drying Sails, André Derain, 1905

This work will never be finished!
A huge pile of candy is there to
be shared. Visitors to the gallery are
allowed to help themselves. At the
end of the day, the pile of candy can
be completely restocked.

The artwork can be understood as
showing the good and bad sides of
sharing. We share friendship, but we
might also catch each other's colds!

We're all equal, just like these
candies wrapped in shiny paper. With
this artwork the artist makes us think
about life, and how it constantly
changes, just like this pile of candy.

MADE FOR SHARING

"Untitled" (USA Today), Felix Gonzalez-Torres, 1990

WHAT is it EXACTLY?

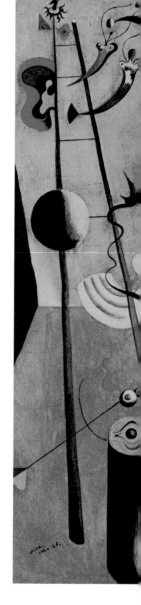

In some art it's difficult to know what we're LOOKING AT.

Artists can change objects and people to make them **unrecognizable**. Or they can make art about things that are completely **made up** and not from the world around us at all. This is called **abstract art**. Even experts can get confused. Some abstract art has been **displayed upside down** for ages before anyone realized! Abstract artists have decided that they shouldn't have to try to copy things from the world, but can **make up** whatever they like.

WHERE is Harlequin? CLUE: he has a guitar, a mustache, a beard, a hat and a pipe.

The Harlequin's Carnival, Joan Miró, 1924-25

The **first abstract artists** decided
to paint shapes and colors that don't
represent anything from the real
world. Artists like **Joan Miró** painted
unconsciously, which is painting
without thinking about it.

Miró went into a kind of **trance** when
he painted. Although he knew what he
was doing, he was in a sort of dream.
This is an **abstract work** of art, but the
strange shapes mean something to Miró.

Is it good
or is it bad?
Go to page 80

FLYING FISH!

Alexander Calder developed a special way of bending and twisting wire to create his 3D "drawings in space," or mobiles.

This standing mobile sways and moves gently in the air like fish swimming through water. A lot of abstract art, like this example, shows things from the world in a different way. Other abstract art doesn't even pretend to be part of the world we know.

Steel Fish. Alexander Calder, 1934

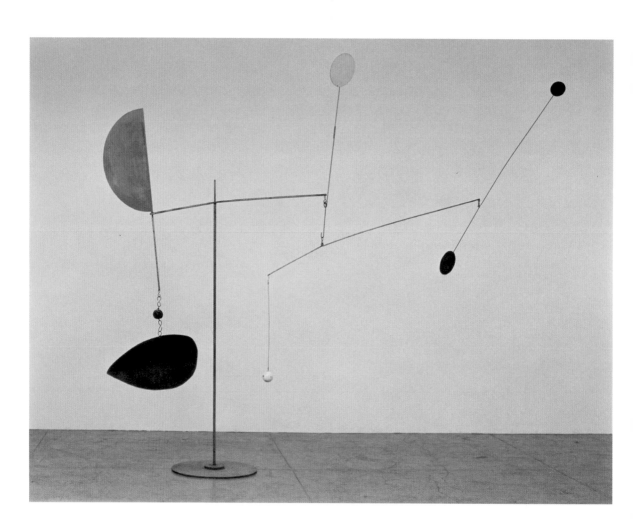

MYSTERIES FROM HISTORY

Aboriginal artists in Australia have made abstract art for centuries. Their art tells us about ancient beliefs. All the colors and shapes are telling mysterious stories about the Aborigines' ancestors who lived long ago. The art is meant to look flat and pattern-like, and only suggest things from the real world.

Warnampi Tingari, Dick Tjupurrula, 1980

DOES **THIS LOOK LIKE** YOUR FAMILY?

Barbara Hepworth liked to carve the shapes she saw in the Cornish landscape where she lived. Although this might not look like a family group, Hepworth has used the shapes she loves to suggest a family.

Which one's the mom? You see, you know the answer! That's what a lot of abstract art is about. It suggests things that we all understand, even without us actually seeing them.

Three Spheres (Family Group),
Barbara Hepworth, 1972

Is it upside down?

LOOK →

Is it the
right way
up? How do
you know?

Picasso and his friend Braque were always EXPERIMENTING with new ways of painting.

In the early 1900s, they started an art movement called **Cubism**. Cubists painted objects from many **different perspectives**, or angles, all **in the same picture**.

Cubists felt they were showing more of everything with their special method. But this could make it **difficult to understand** their pictures!

What is it exactly?
Go to page 56

Some **Cubists** put little **clues** in their pictures to help people **understand** them. This painting by Georges Braque is all about **searching for clues**.

The stenciled letters and numbers were Braque's way of showing **which way up** his Cubist painting should be. They also show that it is a painting on a flat surface. This was another part of Cubism – to be clear that it was art and **not part of the real world**.

The Portuguese. Georges Braque, 1911

60

Jackson Pollock dripped, splashed and threw paint all over his canvas to make this work of art. He started by laying a huge blank canvas on the floor, and then worked from all sides as he let his feelings pour out with the paint. So if he worked from every side and it's not supposed to be anything we recognize, is there a right way up?

WHICH WAY?

Drip painting 27. Jackson Pollock, 1950

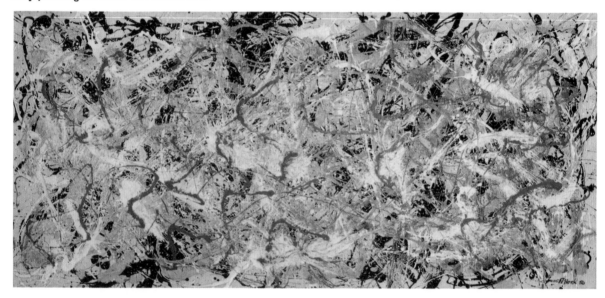

IN A SPIN!

This painting spins round on the wall. It has no right way up and is never upside down!

Inspired by memories of a simple painting technique that he saw as a child on a TV programe, Damien Hirst began making spin paintings to show that skill is not as important as ideas in art.

Beautiful, amore, gasp, eyes going into the top of the head and fluttering painting. Damien Hirst, 1997

Robert Delaunay painted circles of bright colors to create the idea of rhythm and movement. His bold shapes and contrasting colors are powerful. Some people even think Delaunay's paintings give us music without sounds!

Look at the picture for a long time. Do the circles seem to dance? Can you imagine what this painting might sound like? Does it matter which way up it is?

CAN YOU SEE THE RHYTHM?

Rythme, Joie de Vivre. Robert Delaunay, 1931

THAT'S just WEIRD!

HOW→

many flowers, vegetables and pieces of fruit can you count?

Over 400 years ago, **Giuseppe Arcimboldo** painted in a way that was really **original**. This is his portrait of an emperor!

He called this painting *Vertumnus* after an ancient Roman god. Fruit and vegetables were **expensive**, so they **symbolize** the **riches** that the emperor had created for his people. All of Arcimboldo's portraits are made up of **unusual** things such as vegetables, fruit and even kitchen utensils. At the time people were **fascinated** by **puzzles** and the **bizarre**.

Art can be WEIRD. It can be wacky, confusing and even scary!

That's because many artists explore and **express their ideas in unusual ways**. Some artists make their work like **riddles** for us to work out. Others make peculiar-looking art to make us **think in different ways**, and some artworks look like they could be dreams or nightmares.

What's with all the fruit?
Go to page 36

Vertumnus, Giuseppe Arcimboldo, c. 1590-91

DON'T PUT YOUR TEA IN THIS!

A tea cup, saucer and spoon covered in fur? It's odd, but it is the sort of thing you might see in your dreams.

Meret Oppenheim wanted to be unexpected and to surprise us. She was part of the Surrealist movement that explored dreams and subconscious thoughts.

Object. Meret Oppenheim. 1936

A FLYING TRAIN?

Surrealists were interested in the subconscious, the part of our brains where our memories are stored.

This is a weird arrangement of objects in the wrong sizes and in the wrong places.

It was meant to hang on a wall at the bottom of a staircase so that the train would look like it was coming towards people as they passed. René Magritte was showing that no matter how realistically something is painted, it is only ever pretend, and things can happen in art that wouldn't be possible in real life.

Time Transfixed. René Magritte, 1938

Berndnaut Smilde creates clouds inside rooms. He uses special equipment to make dramatic and realistic clouds.

The clouds are all different and they only last for a few moments before they disappear. So Smilde takes photos of them.

His idea is to create something that is in between real and pretend. His creations look like the real, fluffy clouds in the sky, but they are smaller and made to appear in unexpected places.

HOW DO YOU GET a cloud INSIDE A ROOM?

Nimbus Dumont, Berndnaut Smilde, 2014

DO ARTISTS COPY each other?

Pope Innocent X, Diego Velázquez, 1650

A common way for an artist to learn how to be an artist is to COPY somebody else's work.

But once someone is a real artist, they need to be more **original**.

Many painters use other painters' **ideas** to create their own work. They might change the **style**, or use the same **composition**, or arrangement, with a different **subject**. Occasionally, these "copies" have become as **famous** as the original works of art. Some artists have been **inspired** by other things, too, such as TV or newspapers.

Study after Velázquez's Portrait of Pope Innocent X, 1953.
Francis Bacon, 1953

For over twenty years, Francis Bacon made **many variations** of Velázquez's portrait of Pope Innocent X, even though he'd never seen the actual painting.

Bacon's painting of the pope is **distorted**. He has made him look see-through and as if he's **trapped** in a glass box, **screaming**.

WHAT is the same and what is different?

Sazai Hall at the Temple of the Five Hundred Arhats (Gohyakurakanji Sazaido), from the series Thirty-Six Views of Mount Fuji, Hokusai, c. 1830-33

Garden at Sainte-Adresse, Claude Monet, 1867

Claude Monet loved this print by the Japanese artist Hokusai. At the time, many French Impressionist artists were interested in Japanese art. They liked the simple arrangements, flat colors and flowing lines.

In Hokusai's print, people look across to Mount Fuji from a pavillion. Monet's composition of his aunt's garden is similar. Monet's people are the same distance from the ship on the horizon as the figures in Hokusai's print are from Mount Fuji.

Andy Warhol believed that we have become obsessed with celebrities. He thought that newspapers, films and TV encouraged this. After the film star Marilyn Monroe died in August 1962, Warhol made more than twenty prints of her, all based on a photo of her from a film.

Warhol's images are brightly colored on one side, but black and white on the other, suggesting life and death.

By repeating the copied photograph so many times, he was echoing how obsessed the press was with Marilyn Monroe.

Marilyn Diptych. Andy Warhol, 1962

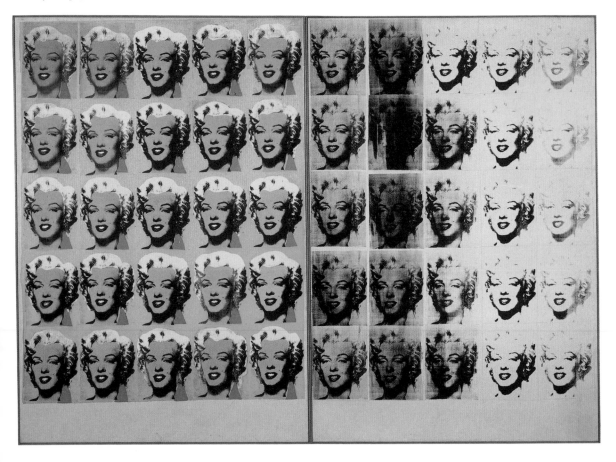

My little SISTER COULD DO THAT!

HOW➡ does this picture make you feel?

Is it finished?
Go to page 52

Do you ever think a work of art looks as though you could have done it yourself?

Some art seems so **simple** that you might wish you'd thought of it first. But often artists' **concepts**, or **ideas**, are more **complicated** than they look.

By the end of the 1800s, many artists didn't see the point of **realistic** painting or drawing any more. The **camera** had been invented and could capture a scene exactly. Art became more about **ideas** than about being lifelike. Artists were inspired by many things, including **children's drawings**. They concentrated on drawing their ideas instead of making their pictures **realistic**.

The Snail. Henri Matisse, 1953

Have you ever made a picture by cutting out **paper shapes** and sticking them down? That's what **Henri Matisse** did in this collage when he was 83 years old.

Although it might **look simple**, it's not! Matisse knew a great deal about **colors, shapes, balance** and **proportions**, and what affects our moods. He wanted to make art that is **soothing, calming** and **happy**, like "a comfortable armchair."

Jean-Michel Basquiat painted energetically and with few details, just as a young child might. He wasn't trying to show off his artistic skills, but was trying to paint how he felt at that moment. Basquiat painted in a strong, passionate way with slashing, colorful, messy marks that can look a little bit frightening.

HOW DO YOU THINK HE FELT?

Boy and Dog in a Johnnypump. Jean-Michel Basquiat, 1982

MAKE YOUR OWN PET!

Joseph Cornell produced lots of art by cutting things out, finding objects and arranging them together in boxes. He created imaginary, dreamlike worlds to make us look at familiar things with fresh eyes.

What does this remind you of? It made Cornell think of his childhood, when he used to see exotic birds for sale in his local pet shop.

A Parrot for Juan Gris. Joseph Cornell, 1953-54

74

Far in front of you, stretching on through the gallery, is a crowd of thousands of tiny clay figures, all looking straight at you. Designed by the sculptor Antony Gormley, each one is about the size of a hand. They're so simple-looking, they could almost have been made by anyone.

But the idea behind them is not at all childlike. They make us think about everyone living together in the world.

EUROPEAN FIELD. Installation view, Kunsthalle zu Kiel, Kiel, Germany, Antony Gormley, 1993

CAN YOU *SEE* WHAT THEY ARE?

WHY iS ART SO EXPENSIVE?

REALLY?

In 1987, this sold for the highest known price ever paid privately for a painting!

It's crazy! Some works of art cost MILLIONS and others not much at all.

Why? It's all about how much people **want** something and how **rare** it is. Artists and styles can go in and out of **fashion**.

Today Vincent van Gogh is really famous and his paintings sell for **millions**. But when he was **alive**, he only sold one painting! Only after he died did people want his work. The artist being **dead** often helps to make their art more **valuable**!

Vincent van Gogh painted sunflowers often. He painted this picture for his guest room when the artist **Paul Gauguin** came to stay. The visit ended in an **argument**, Gauguin left, and Van Gogh **cut off** part of his own **ear**. The famous **story** behind this painting has helped to **increase its value**.

Sunflowers. Vincent van Gogh, 1888

Do you know about Banksy? He's a graffiti artist who paints on walls and sidewalks when no one else is looking. His art makes people think about things that are happening in the world. It's thoughtful and lifelike and admired by many. Lots of people would like to own his art and are prepared to pay a lot of money for it. But how do you own paintings that are on buildings or the sidewalk?

Banksy sometimes sells his art and occasionally puts on exhibitions, but his art is still hard to get — and expensive to buy.

Maid in London. Banksy, 2006

PRICE-LESS!

Some art is so valuable that it can't be given a price. It is priceless! Johannes Vermeer's paintings are this precious.

In his lifetime Vermeer produced just a few pictures. He painted slowly and carefully using very expensive paints. This portrait is so highly prized, it's sometimes called the "Dutch Mona Lisa." No one knows who the girl in the picture was, but her wide watching eyes and large, shiny pearl earring show Vermeer's special method of painting color and light.

Girl with a Pearl Earring, Johannes Vermeer, 1665

MONEY OR ART?

When Andy Warhol printed colorful images of the American dollar sign, he was effectively printing money. Warhol was always interested in how we spend money and value things. He found it fascinating that he could copy a symbol of money to make art that ended up being worth lots and lots of money!

Dollar Signs, Andy Warhol, 1981

IS it GOOD or is it BAD?

Is a canvas splashed with paint as GOOD as a realistic painting from centuries ago?

Art can be baffling sometimes, especially if it isn't lifelike.

From the late 1800s, artists began to make **abstract art**, or art that doesn't look like things from the world around us. They used **unusual materials**, colors, shapes and forms. Artists wanted to **experiment** and **test people's reactions**.

This changed opinions about what is **good** and what is **bad art**.

WHERE →
has the firework just exploded in the sky?

James Abbott McNeill Whistler wanted to show an **atmosphere** rather than lifelike details in this painting of fireworks on a misty night.

The **art critic** John Ruskin was **horrified**. He said that this wasn't **"proper art"** and accused Whistler of "flinging a pot of paint in the public's face."

The public listened to Ruskin and decided that Whistler's art was rubbish. But **opinions change**. Today, Whistler is seen as a **great artist**.

Nocturne in Black and Gold (The Falling Rocket), James Abbott McNeill Whistler, 1875

Henri Rousseau's painting of the jungle doesn't look realistic. So is it bad?

Rousseau taught himself to paint by copying pictures from books, and the wild trees and vegetation are studies of pot plants made to look huge. By painting each leaf and simplifying the tiger, Rousseau made his picture look flat like a collage, with no perspective or realism. His rich colors and dark and bright areas add to the unreal effect.

Picasso was inspired by Rousseau's simplified style, which is called "Naïve art."

HOW DO YOU IMAGINE THE JUNGLE?

Surprised! Henri Rousseau, 1891

A PAINTING OR STAINED GLASS?

Paul Gauguin believed that people looking at his art should understand what it is about without having to think very hard, so he used strong colors and shapes to create atmosphere. His paintings look like colorful stained glass. People hated them at first because they didn't look realistic, but now his work is much admired.

Vision after the Sermon. Paul Gauguin, 1888

BUT IT'S A TOILET!

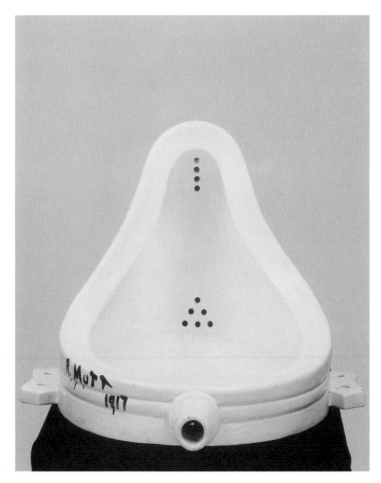

How could anyone put a urinal on display and say it is a work of art? In 1917, that's exactly what Marcel Duchamp did. Everyone who saw it was shocked.

Duchamp argued that an artist doesn't have to make something to exhibit it. He said that art should be about ideas. He wanted people to look at objects in new ways, and especially to value original ideas even more than artistic skill.

Fountain. Marcel Duchamp, 1917

DO YOU HAVE to be CLEVER to look at ART?

FIND →

a tiny ornament of Jesus on the cross. It shows that both men were Catholic.

Some people think that you have to be clever to UNDERSTAND art.

Others think that art can make you **clever**. But most of the time you just have to know **what to look for.**

If art was made a long time ago, it might contain things that we don't recognize now. Sometimes we just need to look carefully and try to **work out** what we think the artists might have **meant.** Lots of works of art have **clues** to help us work out what's going on. Some have even been made to **teach us things**.

The **more you study** this picture, the more you'll **see**. Look at the **objects** between the two men. The globes of the Earth and the stars tell us that they were **well-traveled** and **well-educated**.

On the floor is a squashed **skull**. Hold this book near to your left eye and you'll see it. Hans Holbein reminds us that life doesn't last **forever**.

The Ambassadors. Hans Holbein the Younger, 1533

Find some weird art!
Go to page 64

CAN YOU LEARN AN OLD SKILL?

Court Ladies Preparing Newly Woven Silk,
attributed to Emperor Huizong, early 1100s

Made in ancient China, this delicate painting shows ladies preparing newly woven silk. It's an old skill that most people no longer know about, but if you study the painting, you can learn how to do it! Paintings like this are like detailed how-to diagrams.

PICTURES TO MAKE YOU CLEVER!

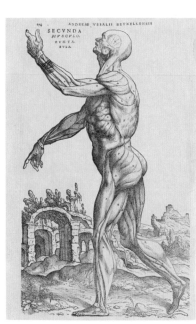

Andreas Vesalius was a doctor and an illustrator. In 1543, he illustrated seven books for doctors to study. He cut up dead human bodies to examine the organs and make sure that his pictures were accurate.

Before this time, people learned about how the body works by cutting up animals, not humans. These pictures were revolutionary!

De Humani Corporis Fabrica Libri Septem,
Andreas Vesalius, 1543

You need to know about ancient myths to work out what's happening in this picture. It's a complicated scene from a Greek myth. When it was painted, only educated people knew the tale and the characters in it. Titian had to read the myth carefully before he started to paint.

The man on the chariot is a Greek god called Bacchus. He's about to leap off his chariot to talk to Ariadne, the girl waving to a ship in the distance that has just left her stranded on this island.

Bacchus and Ariadne. Titian, 1520-23

WHY do I have TO BE QUIET in a GALLERY?

WHAT do you think these colors sound like?

SHH! Be quiet! The artworks are talking!

Have you ever been told to be quiet in an art gallery? It's because the artworks themselves have a lot to say.

Art is full of ideas, **messages** and stories. So being quiet in front of an artwork can help you **concentrate** on what it has to tell you. If you're quiet you can also discover a lot more in the art for yourself.

Improvisation Gorge. Wassily Kandinsky, 1914

Wassily Kandinsky believed that his paintings were like **music**. He thought that yellow sounded like trumpets, light blue like a flute, dark blue like a cello and black, a dramatic pause. He had something called **"synaesthesia,"** which meant that he could **"see" sounds** and **"hear" colors.**

Another good reason to be **quiet in a gallery** is so you can hear Kandinsky's colors!

Why is everything blurry?
Go to page 44

SHOW SOME RESPECT!

This is a miniature painting of a meeting house built long ago by the Mughal Emperor Akbar.

The artist, Nar Singh, has painted men from different faiths sitting quietly together in harmony. Viewers of the painting are expected to be quiet and peaceful, too, to show respect for the different religious groups present.

It was unusual and difficult for Emperor Akbar to bring all these religious people together. The painting was made in honor of his peace-making skills.

Jesuits at Akbar's Court. Nar Singh, c. 1605

ARE YOU SITTING QUIETLY?

This painting was made by Mark Rothko to hang in a restaurant in New York. But as he painted, he decided that he wanted his work to be where people would concentrate on it — not on their food and friends. So he gave it to the Tate gallery in London, saying that viewers should sit and enjoy the colors and shapes in peace.

Red on Maroon. Mark Rothko, 1959

You don't always have to be quiet to enjoy art! Niki de Saint Phalle made this sculpture especially for children to play on. It is a monster and has three red tongues to slide down.

You may have to be quiet in galleries and museums, but you can be as loud as you like around this open-air work.

The Golem. Niki de Saint Phalle, 1972

(((BE AS LOUD))) AS YOU LIKE!

GLOSSARY

abstract art Art that is not realistic — it doesn't look like anything from the world around us. Abstract art is often based on shapes, lines and colors to create moods.

art critic A person who writes or talks about art, judging how good or bad it is.

art movement A style of art made at a particular time. Impressionism and Pop art are examples of art movements.

cast A sculpture made from a mold. It is a way of making an exact copy of one design.

circa (c.) A Latin word for "about." Before a date, c. means "on about that date."

collage A picture made with paper or other materials that are glued on to a surface.

composition The arrangement of the parts of a picture.

conceptual art Art of the imagination, or art made from artists' ideas.

Cubism A style of art developed in the 1900s where artists wanted to paint 3D things on flat surfaces in a new, descriptive way. So they painted objects and people from several different angles at once.

forms (3D shapes) For instance, a square is a shape, a cube is its form; a circle is a shape, a ball or sphere is its form.

graffiti art This started in the 1970s with brightly colored spray-painted images that were made on buildings and in other public places. Today graffiti art is also made for galleries and museums.

Impressionism An art style that recreates the light and colors we see in quick, passing moments. It was developed by a group of artists in the 1860s and 1870s.

installation A three-dimensional work of art that is designed for a particular space.

landscape A work of art that features the outside world, such as the sea, mountains, lakes, rivers, gardens, towns and cities.

life drawing Drawing the nude, or naked people. It is how most art students have learned to draw for hundreds of years.

mobile A type of sculpture that is hung from above. It has attached shapes or figures that move easily in the air.

naïve art Art that often seems childlike or simple, but might have extra hidden meanings.

narrative Telling a story.

Op art A type of abstract art that creates optical (of the eye) illusions of movement with lines and patterns.

open air painting To paint in the open air, in front of the scene the artist is painting.

painting A flat artwork on a canvas, panel or wall completed using paint.

performance artist An artist who acts out artistic ideas rather than making a sculpture or a painting.

perspective A way of showing things that are three-dimensional on a flat, or 2D, surface to make them look 3D.

petroglyph Drawings or carvings on rocks, usually made hundreds or even thousands of years ago.

pixels Tiny dots that form the pictures on TV screens and computer monitors.

pointillism A way of painting using only small dots of pure colors to create entire paintings. It was invented by Georges Seurat and Paul Signac in 1886.

Pop art Making art using ideas from popular culture, or things we all know about, such as magazines, comics, TV and films. This "popular" or "pop" art began in the 1950s and became fashionable in the 1960s.

portrait A drawing or painting of a person. It might include the whole body or just the face.

proportion The connection of one thing to another in terms of size and distance.

realism A style of painting in which the artist wants everything they paint to appear lifelike and believable.

sculpture 3D art, usually made by carving or molding materials such as clay, bronze or marble.

self-portrait A portrait made by an artist of him or herself.

still life A work of art of things that do not or cannot move, such as furniture, fruit or flowers.

stylized Something that is created in an unnatural style to make it look perfect or different.

subject What a work of art is about.

Surrealism A style of art that began in the 1920s when some artists began to paint or sculpt dreams and other ideas from their subconscious minds rather than what they saw in front of them.

synaesthesia A condition that some people have where in their heads, they might "see" sounds and "hear" colors.

three-dimensional Something with depth, height and width, also called 3D.

tone Shadows, dark and light colors that are created by light or lack of it.

two-dimensional Flat surfaces with no depth, such as a piece of paper, also called 2D.

INDEX

LIST OF ILLUSTRATIONS

Dimensions are given in cm (inches); height before width.

a = above
b = below
c = centre

4a, 23b Amedeo Modigliani, *Woman with a fan*, 1919. Oil on canvas, 100 x 65 (36 3/8 x 25 5/8). Musée d'Art Moderne de la Ville de Paris **4b, 22** Sophie Taeuber-Arp, *Untitled*, 1932. Gouache on paper. Private Collection/Bridgeman Images **4c, 82** Henri Rousseau, *Surprised!*, 1891. Oil on canvas, 129.8 x 161.9 (51 1/8 x 63 3/4). National Gallery, London **6** Rembrandt, *Belshazzar's Feast*, 1636-38. Oil on canvas, 167.6 x 209.2 (66 x 82 3/8) National Gallery, London **7a** Edvard Munch, *The Scream*, 1893. Tempera and crayon on cardboard, 91 x 73.5 (35 7/8 x 29 1/8). Munch Museum, Oslo **7b** Kazimir Malevich, *Suprematist Composition,* 1916. Oil on canvas, 88.5 x 71 (34 7/8 x 28). Private collection **9** Rock painting from Utah, USA. Late Ute Indian style, c.150 CE. Natural pigments on rock. Photo © Fred and Randi Hirschmann/ SuperStock/Corbis **10a** Keith Haring, *Untitled,* 1982. Acrylic on aluminium, 228.6 x 182.9 (90 x 72). Christie's Images, London/Scala, Florence. © Keith Haring Estate **10b** L.S. Lowry, *Going to Work*, 1959. Watercolor on paper, 27 x 38.5 (10 5/8 x 15 1/8). © The Lowry Collection, Salford **11** Alberto Giacometti, *Man Pointing*, 1947. Bronze, 179 x 103.4 x 41.5 (70 1/2 x 40 3/4 x 16 3/8). Museum of Modern Art, New York. © The Estate of Alberto Giacometti (Fondation Giacometti, Paris and ADAGP, Paris), licensed in the UK by ACS and DACS, London 2016 **13** Artist unknown, *Discobolus Lancellotti*, Roman copy after a bronze original by Myron (460-450 BC). Marble, h. 156 cm (61 3/8). Museo Nazionale Romano, Palazzo Massimo alle Terme, Rome **14a** Karel Appel, *Mouse on Table*, 1971. Aluminium with automobile enamel. Private Collection/Photo Boltin Picture Library/Bridgeman Images. © Karel Appel Foundation/DACS 2016 **14b** Picasso, *Head of a Woman*, 1962. Metal, paint, 32 x 24 x 16 (12 5/8 x 9 1/2 x 6 ¼). Musée Picasso, Paris. © Succession Picasso/DACS, London 2016 **15** Henry Moore, *Recumbent Figure*, 1938. Green Hornton stone, 132.7 x 88.9 x 73.7 (52 1/4 x 35 x 29). Tate, London. Reproduced by permission of The Henry Moore Foundation **17** Piet Mondrian, *Composition with Yellow, Red, Black, Blue, and Gray*, 1920. Oil on canvas, 51.5 x 61 (20 1/4 x 24). Stedelijk Museum,

Amsterdam **18** Georges Seurat, *A Sunday afternoon on the island of La Grande Jatte*, 1884. Oil on canvas, 207.5 x 308.1 (81 3/4 x 121 1/4). Art Institute of Chicago. Helen Birch Bartlett Memorial Collection (1926.224) **19a** Frida Kahlo, *The Frame*, 1938. Oil on aluminum, reverse painting on glass and painting frame, 28.5 x 20.7 (11 1/4 x 8 1/8). Centre Georges Pompidou, Musée national d'art moderne, Paris. State purchase and attribution, 1939 (T2011.206.48). © 2016. Banco de México Diego Rivera Frida Kahlo Museums Trust, Mexico, D.F./DACS **19b** Simone Martini and Lippo Memmi, *Annunciation with St Margaret and St Ansanus*, 1333. Tempera and gold on panel, 305 x 265 (120 x 104). Uffizi, Florence **21** *Nebamun fowling in the marshes*, Tomb-chapel of Nebamun, c.1350 BCE, 18th Dynasty, Thebes. Paint on plaster, 83 x 98 (32 5/8 x 38 5/8). British Museum, London **23** Jean Metzinger, *Table by a window*, 1917. Oil on canvas, 81.3 x 65.4 (32 x 25 3/4). Metropolitan Museum of Art, New York. Purchase, The M. L. Annenberg Foundation, Joseph H. Hazen Foundation Inc., and Joseph H. Hazen Gifts, 1959 (59.86). © ADAGP, Paris and DACS, London 2016 **25** Sandro Botticelli, *The Birth of Venus*, 1486. Tempera on canvas, 172 x 278 (67 3/4 x 109 1/2). Uffizi, Florence **26a** Yves Klein, *Untitled Anthropometry*, 1960. Pure pigment and synthetic resin on paper laid down on canvas. © Yves Klein, ADAGP, Paris and DACS, London 2016 **26b** Grant Wood, *American Gothic*, 1930. Oil on beaver board, 78 x 65.3 (30 3/4 x 25 ¾. Art Institute of Chicago. Friends of American Art Collection (1930.934) **27** Édouard Manet, *Le Dejeuner sur l'Herbe*, 1863. Oil on canvas, 208 x 264.5 (81 7/8 x 104 1/8). Musée d'Orsay, Paris **29** John Everett Millais, *Ophelia*, 1851-52. Oil paint on canvas, 76.2 x 111.8 (30 x 44). Tate, London **30** Cornelia Parker, *Cold Dark Matter: An Exploded View*, 1991. A garden shed and contents blown up for the artist by the British Army, the fragments suspended around a light bulb. Tate, London. Courtesy the artist and Frith Street Gallery, London. © Cornelia Parker **31a** Scene from *The Bayeux Tapestry*, c.1070. Wool embroidered linen, overall c.50 x 7000 (20 in. x 231 feet). The Bayeux Tapestry Museum, Normandy, France **31b** Sofonisba Anguissola, *The Chess Game*, 1555. Oil on canvas, 72 x 97 (28 3/8 x 38 1/8). National Museum, Pozna, Poland **33** Diego Velázquez, *Las Meninas*, 1656. Oil on canvas, 318 x 276 (125.2 x 108.7). Museo del Prado, Madrid **34** Edward Hopper, *Chop Suey*, 1929. Oil on canvas, 81.3 x 96.5 (32

x 38). Collection of Barney A. Ebsworth **35a** Caravaggio, *David with the head of Goliath*, 1610. Oil on canvas, 125 x 101 (49 x 40). Galleria Borghese, Rome **35b** Marc Quinn, *Self*, 2006. Blood (artist's), stainless steel, perspex and refrigeration equipment, 208 x 63 x 63 (81 7/8 x 24 3/4 x 24 3/4). Courtesy Marc Quinn Studio **37** Paul Cezanne, *Apples and Oranges*, 1899. Oil on canvas, 74 x 93 (29 1/8 x 36 5/8). Musée d'Orsay, Paris **38** Ori Gerscht, *Blow up 05*, 2007. Photograph © Ori Gerscht **39a** Jan van Kessel, *Vanitas Still Life*, 1665-70. Oil on copper, 20.3 x 15.2 (8 x 6). National Gallery of Art, Washington, D.C. Gift of Maida and George Abrams (1995.74.2) **39b** Johan Lorbeer, *Tarzan/Standing Leg*, 2002. Still Life Performance, 2 hours. Photo H. Hermes. © Johan Lorbeer **41** Caspar David Friedrich, *Wanderer Above the Sea of Fog*, 1818. Oil on canvas, 95 x 75 (37 3/8 x 29 1/2). Kunsthalle Hamburg **42a** David Hockney, *The Arrival of Spring in Woldgate, East Yorkshire in 2011 (twenty eleven) - 2 January*. iPad drawing printed on paper, 139.7 x 105.4 (55 x 41 1/2). Edition of 25. © David Hockney **42b** Christo and Jeanne-Claude, *Surrounded Islands, Biscayne Bay, Greater Miami, Florida, 1980-83*. Photo Wolfgang Volz. © Copyright Christo 1983 **43** *Wheatfield - A Confrontation: Battery Park Landfill, Downtown Manhattan*, with Agnes Denes standing in the field, 1982. Photo John McGrail. Courtesy Leslie Tonkonow Artworks + Projects, New York **45** Berthe Morisot, *In the Dining Room*, 1886. Oil on canvas, 61.3 x 50 (24 1/8 x 19 11/16). National Gallery of Art, Washington, D.C. Chester Dale Collection (1963.10.185) **46** J.W.M. Turner, *Steamboat Off a Harbour's Mouth*, 1842. Oil on canvas, 91.4 x 121.9 (36 x 48). Tate, London **47a** Gerhard Richter, *Reisebüro Tourist Office*, 1966. Oil on canvas, 150 x 130 (59 x 51 1/8). © Gerhard Richter 2016 **47b** Meredith Frampton, *A Game of Patience (Miss Margaret Austin-Jones)*, 1937. Oil on canvas, 106.7 x 78.7 (42 x 31). Ferens Art Gallery, Hull Museums. © The Trustees of the Meredith Frampton Estate **49** Yayoi Kusama, *With All My Love For The Tulips, I Pray Forever*, 2012. Courtesy KUSAMA Enterprise, Ota Fine Arts, Tokyo/Singapore and Victoria Miro, London. © Yayoi Kusama **50a** Georges Seurat, *Young Woman Powdering Herself*, 1889-90. Oil on canvas, 95.5 x 79.5 (37 5/8 x 31 1/4). The Samuel Courtauld Trust, The Courtauld Gallery, London **50b** Bridget Riley, *Pause*, 1964. Emulsion on hardboard, 112.2 x 106.5 (44 1/8 x 41 3/4). © Bridget Riley 2016.

Text by Susie Hodge
Original illustrations by Claire Goble
Edited by Sue Grabham
Designed by Anna Perotti at By The Sky Design
Original concept by Alice Harman

First published in 2016 in hardcover in
the United States of America by
Thames & Hudson Inc., 500 Fifth Avenue,
New York, New York 10110

thamesandhudsonusa.com

Library of Congress Catalog Card Number
2016931241

ISBN 978-0-500-65080-6

Printed and bound in China by Everbest
Printing Co. Ltd